soup

THE AUSTRALIAN
Women's Weekly

contents

Soups are practical and economical, but the real bonus is, they're nutritious. You can warm the family up *and* sneak in a few more vegies. All the soups in this book can be made tonight to eat tonight, or flip to our storage tips for freezing information. You'll love these delicious, quick modern recipes.

Pamela Clark

Editorial & food director

Australian cup and spoon measurements are metric. A conversion chart appears on page 77.

30 minutes

Perfect for busy bodies, here is a delicious collection of soups that can be on the table in half an hour. Plus, these soups are packed with nutritious ingredients — you'll feel fuller for longer.

chicken, corn & noodle soup

- 1 tablespoon vegetable oil
- 1 medium brown onion (150g), chopped finely
- 2 cloves garlic, crushed
- 3cm (1¼-inch) piece fresh ginger (15g), grated
- 1 litre (4 cups) chicken stock
- 2 cups (500ml) water
- 125g (4 ounces) canned creamed corn
- 420g (13½ ounces) canned corn kernels, rinsed, drained
- 125g (4 ounces) dried wheat noodles
- 350g (11 ounces) chicken breast fillets, sliced thinly
- 2 tablespoons japanese soy sauce
- 100g (3 ounces) baby spinach leaves
- 4 green onions (scallions), chopped coarsely

1 Heat oil in a large saucepan over medium heat; cook brown onion, garlic and ginger, stirring, 5 minutes or until onion softens.

2 Add stock, the water, creamed corn and corn kernels to the pan; cover, bring to the boil over high heat.

3 Reduce heat to low-medium; simmer, uncovered, for 5 minutes.

4 Carefully break the noodles in half and add to the pan. Simmer, uncovered, for 2 minutes. Stir to separate noodles.

5 Add chicken to the pan with soy sauce; simmer, uncovered, 1 minute or until chicken is cooked through. Add extra soy sauce to taste, if needed.

6 Stir in spinach; season to taste. Using a ladle, divide the soup between bowls. Sprinkle with green onion.

serves 4
prep + cook time 30 minutes
nutritional count per serving 7.8g total fat (1.5g saturated fat); 1664kJ (398 cal); 47.9g carbohydrate; 30.7g protein; 6.3g fibre

tip Diced fresh vegetable soup mix consists of carrot, onion and celery that has been chopped and packaged for your convenience. It creates a good base for many vegetable soups and is a great time-saver. It can be found in the chilled lettuce section of major supermarkets.

bacon, vegetable & red lentil soup

- 1 tablespoon olive oil
- 400g (12½-ounce) packet diced fresh vegetable soup mix (see tip)
- 2 cloves garlic, crushed
- 3 rindless bacon slices (195g), chopped finely
- 1 cup (200g) red lentils
- 1 litre (4 cups) salt-reduced chicken stock
- 2 tablespoons coarsely chopped chives
- 2 tablespoons coarsely chopped fresh flat-leaf parsley
- 1 tablespoon finely chopped fresh tarragon

1 Heat oil in a large saucepan over high heat; add soup mix, garlic and bacon, stirring, until vegetables soften. Add lentils and stock; bring to the boil, simmer, stirring occasionally, for 15 minutes or until lentils are tender and soup has thickened.
2 Serve soup sprinkled with herbs. Accompany with fresh crusty bread rolls, if you like.

serves 4
prep + cook time
30 minutes
nutritional count per serving 13.4g total fat (3.6g saturated fat); 1417kJ (338 cal); 26g carbohydrate; 24.9g protein; 10.2g fibre

hot & sour vegetable soup

- 90g (3 ounces) dried soba noodles
- 1 tablespoon tom yum paste
- 2 kaffir lime leaves, crushed
- 1 long red chilli, halved
- 2 cups (500ml) water
- 2 cups (500ml) chicken stock
- 1 large carrot (180g), cut into matchsticks
- 1 medium red capsicum (bell pepper) (150g), sliced thinly
- 100g (3 ounces) button mushrooms, sliced thinly
- 175g (5½ ounces) broccolini, chopped coarsely
- 100g (3 ounces) snow peas, sliced thinly
- 2 green onions (scallions), sliced thinly
- 1½ tablespoons lime juice
- 1 tablespoon fish sauce
- ½ cup (40g) bean sprouts
- 1 tablespoon fresh mint leaves
- 1 tablespoon fresh coriander leaves (cilantro)

1 Cook noodles in a large saucepan of boiling water until tender; drain.

2 Heat a large non-stick saucepan over medium heat; cook paste, lime leaves and chilli, stirring, until fragrant. Add the water and stock; bring to the boil, while stirring.

3 Reduce heat to low; simmer, uncovered, 5 minutes. Add carrot, capsicum, mushrooms, broccolini and snow peas; simmer, uncovered, 5 minutes or until vegetables are tender.

4 Stir in onion, juice and sauce; season to taste. Discard lime leaves and chilli. Divide noodles between bowls; ladle soup over noodles; top with sprouts and herbs.

serves 2
prep + cook time
25 minutes
nutritional count per
serving 5.4g total fat
(0.7g saturated fat);
1672kJ (400 cal);
59.4g carbohydrate;
21.3g protein; 13.3g fibre

tip Reheat soup in the microwave on HIGH (100%) for 1½ minutes, stirring halfway through heating.

tips This soup can be frozen at the end of step 2. Rouille can be made a day ahead.

fennel & tomato soup with rouille

- 1 medium leek (350g)
- 1 large fennel (550g)
- ¼ cup (60ml) extra virgin olive oil
- 1 medium brown onion (150g), chopped coarsely
- 1 stick celery (150g), trimmed, chopped coarsely
- 3 cloves garlic, crushed
- pinch saffron threads
- 800g (1½ pounds) canned diced tomatoes
- 1 litre (4 cups) vegetable stock
- 2 medium potatoes (400g), cut into 1.5cm (¾-inch) pieces
- 8 x 1.5cm (¾-inch) thick slices sourdough bread (380g)

rouille
- ⅔ cup (200g) whole-egg mayonnaise
- 3 teaspoons lemon juice
- 3 teaspoons tomato paste
- 2 cloves garlic, crushed
- pinch saffron threads
- ¼ teaspoon cayenne pepper

1 Quarter leek lengthways; slice thinly. Reserve fennel tops; chop fennel finely.
2 Heat half the oil in a large saucepan over medium-high heat; cook leek, onion, celery and fennel, stirring, 5 minutes or until softened. Add garlic and saffron; cook, stirring, until fragrant. Add tomatoes, stock and potato; bring to the boil. Reduce heat; simmer, covered, 10 minutes or until tender. Season to taste. Cover to keep hot.
3 Meanwhile, make rouille.

4 Heat a grill pan (or grill or barbecue). Brush bread on both sides with remaining oil; cook until browned lightly on both sides.
5 Ladle soup into serving bowls; top with reserved fennel tops. Serve with toasted bread and rouille.
rouille Combine ingredients in a small bowl; season to taste.

serves 4
prep + cook time 30 minutes
nutritional count per serving 58.3g total fat (9.4g saturated fat); 3825kJ (914 cal); 74.4g carbohydrate; 17.8g protein; 13g fibre

green pea soup with mint pistou

- 1 tablespoon olive oil
- 1 small leek (200g), sliced thinly
- 1 clove garlic, crushed
- 2 large potatoes (600g), chopped coarsely
- 3 cups (360g) frozen peas
- 3 cups (750ml) water
- 2 cups (500ml) vegetable stock

mint pistou

- 2 cups loosely packed fresh mint leaves
- ¼ cup (20g) finely grated parmesan
- 1 tablespoon lemon juice
- 1 clove garlic, quartered
- ¼ cup (60ml) olive oil

1 Heat oil in a large saucepan over medium heat; cook leek and garlic, stirring, for 5 minutes until leek softens. Add potato, peas, the water and stock; bring to the boil. Reduce heat to low; simmer, covered, 10 minutes or until potato is tender. Cool 15 minutes.

2 Meanwhile, make mint pistou.

3 Blend or process soup, in batches, until smooth. Return soup to same cleaned pan; stir over medium heat until hot.

4 Serve bowls of soup topped with pistou.

mint pistou Blend or process ingredients until smooth.

tips This simple and quick soup is made from frozen peas and packaged stock – it's perfect for when you haven't had time to get to the shops. Pistou is a condiment from Provence in France, and is usually made with basil, garlic and olive oil. The word is derived from the Italian 'pestare', to pound. It is similar to Italian pesto. We substituted mint for basil in this recipe.

serves 4
prep + cook time
30 minutes (+ cooling)
nutritional count per serving
20.9g total fat
(3.7g saturated fat); 1634kJ
(391 cal); 32.2g carbohydrate;
12.9g protein; 12g fibre

- ¼ cup (75g) red curry paste
- ½ small cauliflower (500g), chopped coarsely
- 2 medium potatoes (400g), chopped coarsely
- 2 litres (8 cups) water
- 1 tablespoon lime juice

1 Stir curry paste in a heated large saucepan over high heat, for 3 minutes or until fragrant.

2 Add cauliflower, potato and the water; bring to the boil. Reduce heat to low; simmer, uncovered, 15 minutes or until vegetables are tender. Cool 10 minutes.

3 Blend or process soup, in batches, until smooth. Stir in juice; season to taste. Return soup to pan to heat through.

curried cauliflower soup

tip Sprinkle soup with fresh coriander (cilantro) leaves and a pinch of hot paprika.

serves 4
prep + cook time 25 minutes
nutritional count per
serving 7.6g total fat
(0.8g saturated fat); 777kJ
(186 cal); 17.3g carbohydrate;
7.9g protein; 7.2g fibre

serves 4
prep + cook time 25 minutes
nutritional count per serving 20.5g total fat (8.9g saturated fat); 1735kJ (415 cal); 31.6g carbohydrate; 22.8g protein; 7.3g fibre

pork & udon soup

- 1 litre (4 cups) chicken stock
- 2 cups (500ml) water
- 1 red bird's-eye chilli, sliced thinly
- 10cm (4-inch) stick lemon grass (20g), halved lengthways, bruised
- 2 tablespoons japanese soy sauce
- 1 teaspoon sesame oil
- 200g (6½ ounces) fresh udon noodles
- 100g (3 ounces) fresh shiitake mushrooms, sliced thickly
- 230g (7 ounces) canned bamboo shoots, rinsed, drained
- 40g (1½ ounces) baby spinach leaves
- 250g (8 ounces) chinese barbecued pork, sliced thinly

1 Combine stock, the water, chilli and lemon grass in a large saucepan; bring to the boil over high heat. Reduce heat to low-medium; simmer, covered, 5 minutes. Discard lemon grass.

2 Add sauce, oil, noodles, mushrooms and bamboo shoots; simmer, uncovered, 5 minutes. Season to taste.

3 Divide spinach, pork and noodles between bowls; ladle hot soup over the top.

tip Chinese barbecued pork is roasted pork fillet with a sweet, sticky coating. It is available from Asian grocery stores or specialty food shops.

serves 4
prep + cook time 30 minutes
nutritional count per
serving 4.3g total fat
(2.9g saturated fat); 336kJ
(80 cal); 6.2g carbohydrate;
2.9g protein; 2g fibre

dhal with chutney yoghurt

- 1 tablespoon peanut oil
- 1 large brown onion (200g), sliced thinly
- 2cm (¾-inch) piece ginger (10g), grated
- 2 teaspoons brown sugar
- ⅓ cup (75g) korma curry paste
- 1 teaspoon each ground cumin, turmeric and sweet paprika
- 400g (12½ ounces) canned diced tomatoes
- 250g (8 ounces) cherry tomatoes
- 1 cup (250ml) water
- 1 cup (250ml) coconut milk
- 400g (12½ ounces) canned brown lentils, rinsed, drained
- 400g (12½ ounces) canned chickpeas (garbanzo beans), rinsed, drained
- 2 tablespoons coarsely chopped fresh coriander (cilantro)

chutney yoghurt
- ⅔ cup (190g) greek-style yoghurt
- 1 tablespoon mango chutney

1 Heat oil in a large saucepan over medium heat; cook onion, ginger and sugar, stirring, for 3 minutes or until soft. Add curry paste and spices; cook, stirring, 1 minute or until fragrant.
2 Add tomatoes, cherry tomatoes, the water, coconut milk, lentils and chickpeas to pan; bring to the boil. Boil, uncovered, 10 minutes or until thickened slightly. Remove from heat; stand 10 minutes.

3 Meanwhile, make chutney yoghurt.
4 Sprinkle dahl with coriander; serve with chutney yoghurt.

chutney yoghurt
Combine ingredients in a small bowl.

serving suggestion
Serve with warm flat bread.

> **tips** Freeze individual portions of dhal in airtight containers for up to 1 month. Thaw overnight in the fridge; reheat in the microwave. Chutney yoghurt is not suitable to freeze.

greek lima bean soup with fetta & olives

- 2 tablespoons extra virgin olive oil
- 1 large brown onion (200g), chopped coarsely
- 2 medium carrots (240g), chopped coarsely
- 1 stick celery (150g), trimmed, chopped coarsely
- 2 cloves garlic, crushed
- 800g (1½ pounds) canned diced tomatoes
- 1 litre (4 cups) vegetable stock
- 2 cups (500ml) water
- 2 x 400g (12½ ounces) canned lima beans, drained, rinsed
- 2 medium green zucchini (240g), halved lengthways, sliced thinly
- 1 teaspoon finely grated lemon rind
- ⅓ cup (50g) seeded kalamata olives, chopped coarsely
- 100g (3 ounces) greek-style fetta
- 1 tablespoon chopped dill

1 Heat half the oil in a large saucepan over medium heat; cook onion, carrot and celery, stirring, 5 minutes or until softened. Add garlic; cook, stirring, until fragrant.

2 Add tomatoes to pan with stock and the water; bring to the boil. Add beans; simmer, covered, 10 minutes. Add zucchini; simmer, uncovered, about 5 minutes or until tender. Stir in rind; season to taste.

3 Ladle soup into serving bowls; top with olives, crumbled fetta and dill. Drizzle with remaining oil.

serving suggestion
Serve with warm pitta or crusty bread.

tips Large canned lima beans are also known as butter beans. Soup can be frozen at the end of step 2.

serves 6
prep + cook time 30 minutes
nutritional count
per serving 9.7g total fat
(3.4g saturated fat); 815kJ
(195 cal); 14.1g carbohydrate;
9.1g protein; 7.2g fibre

serves 4
prep + cook time 25 minutes
nutritional count
per serving 29.6g total fat
(15.4g saturated fat); 1789kJ
(428 cal); 15.8g carbohydrate;
23.4g protein; 4.3g fibre

chicken laksa

- 1 tablespoon vegetable oil
- 400g (13 ounces) chicken thigh fillets, sliced thinly
- ⅓ cup (100g) laksa paste
- 1½ cups (375ml) chicken stock
- ½ cup (125ml) water
- 1 cup (250ml) coconut milk
- 200g (6½ ounces) bean thread noodles
- ½ cup loosely packed fresh coriander (cilantro) leaves

1 Heat oil in a large saucepan over medium heat, cook chicken, in two batches, turning for 3 minutes, or until browned lightly. Remove from pan.

2 Cook paste in same pan, stirring, 3 minutes or until fragrant. Return chicken to pan with stock, the water and coconut milk; bring to the boil. Reduce heat; simmer, uncovered, 10 minutes or until chicken is cooked. Season to taste.

3 Meanwhile, place noodles in a medium heatproof bowl, cover with boiling water; stand 7 minutes, or until noodles are tender, then drain.

4 Divide noodles between bowls; ladle hot laksa over the top. Serve sprinkled with coriander.

spinach, rocket & pea soup with brie croûtes

- 40g (1½ ounces) butter
- 1 medium leek (350g), sliced
- 1 clove garlic, crushed
- 1 large potato (300g), chopped
- 1 litre (4 cups) vegetable stock
- 1 cup (250ml) water
- 1 cup (120g) frozen peas
- 270g (8½ ounces) spinach, trimmed
- 30g (1 ounce) firmly packed baby rocket (arugula)
- ½ cup (125ml) pouring cream

brie croûtes
- 12 slices (120g) sourdough baguette
- 1 tablespoon dijon mustard
- 150g (4½ ounces) brie cheese

1 Heat butter in a large saucepan over medium heat; cook leek, stirring, 5 minutes or until soft but not coloured. Add garlic; cook, stirring, until fragrant.

2 Add potato, stock and the water to pan; bring to the boil. Reduce heat; simmer, uncovered, 10 minutes or until potato is tender. Add peas, spinach and rocket; simmer, uncovered, 5 minutes. Remove from heat; stand soup 5 minutes.

3 Blend soup in batches until smooth. Return soup to same cleaned pan; stir in cream until hot over medium heat. Season to taste.

4 Meanwhile, make brie croûtes.

5 Ladle soup into serving bowls; serve with croûtes and freshly ground black pepper.

brie croûtes Preheat grill (broiler) to high. Place bread under grill until browned lightly on one side. Turn bread, spread with mustard and top with slices of cheese. Grill until melted slightly.

serves 4
prep + cook time 35 minutes
nutritional count per serving 33.2g total fat (20.4g saturated fat); 2088kJ (500 cal); 29.5g carbohydrate; 18g protein; 7.3g fibre

tips A blender will produce a smoother, finer textured soup than a food processor. This soup is suitable to freeze.

primavera soup with pangrattato

- 30g (1 ounce) butter
- 4 shallots (100g), chopped
- 1 litre (4 cups) vegetable stock
- 2 cups (500ml) water
- ⅓ cup (75g) risoni pasta
- 250g (8 ounces) baby green zucchini, halved lengthways
- 150g (4½ ounces) asparagus, cut into 3cm (1¼-inch) lengths
- 2 cups (240g) frozen baby peas

pangrattato

- 200g (6½ ounces) crusty italian bread
- 2 tablespoons extra virgin olive oil
- 1 fresh long red chilli, sliced thinly
- 2 cloves garlic, chopped
- ⅓ cup loosely packed small flat-leaf parsley leaves
- 1 teaspoon finely grated lemon rind

1 Heat butter in a large saucepan over medium heat; cook shallots, stirring, 3 minutes or until soft.

2 Add stock and the water to pan; bring to the boil. Add pasta and zucchini; simmer, uncovered, 5 minutes, stirring occasionally.

3 Meanwhile, make pangrattato.

4 Add asparagus and peas to soup; simmer, uncovered, 5 minutes or until just tender. Season to taste.

5 Ladle soup into serving bowls; top with pangrattato.

pangrattato Remove crust from bread; tear into 1cm (½-inch) pieces. Heat oil in a large frying pan over medium-high heat; cook chilli and bread pieces, stirring, until browned lightly and crisp. Add garlic; cook until fragrant. Remove from heat; stir in parsley and rind. Season to taste.

serves 4
prep + cook time 25 minutes
nutritional count per serving 17.7g total fat (5.9g saturated fat); 1760kJ (420 cal); 46.7g carbohydrate; 14.3g protein; 9.2g fibre

tips This soup is best made just before serving, as it will discolour on standing. If you can't find baby zucchini, use medium-sized zucchini, sliced thinly. Pangrattato is the Italian word for breadcrumbs.

40 minutes

On a cold winter's night it's hard to go past a hearty soup for dinner. Add a twist to any of these, by topping them with grated parmesan, fresh herbs or a dollop of natural yoghurt.

fish chowder

- **40g (1½ ounces) butter**
- **1 large brown onion (200g), chopped coarsely**
- **1 clove garlic, crushed**
- **2 rindless bacon slices (130g), chopped coarsely**
- **2 tablespoons plain flour**
- **2 medium potatoes (400g), chopped coarsely**
- **3 cups (750ml) milk**
- **2 cups (500ml) vegetable stock**
- **400g (12½ ounces) firm white fish fillets, chopped coarsely**
- **2 tablespoons finely chopped chives**

1 Melt butter in a large saucepan; cook onion, garlic and bacon, stirring, 5 minutes or until onion softens.
2 Add flour; cook, stirring, 1 minute. Add potato, milk and stock; bring to a boil. Reduce heat; simmer, covered, about 10 minutes or until potato is just tender.
3 Add fish; simmer, uncovered, about 4 minutes or until fish is just cooked through. Ladle soup into bowls; sprinkle with chives.
serving suggestion Serve with crusty wholemeal bread.

serves 4
prep + cook time 40 minutes
nutritional count per serving 19.5g total fat (11.6g saturated fat); 1810kJ (433 cal); 28.4g carbohydrate; 34.8g protein; 2.4g fibre

tips Starchy potatoes, such as sebago, are suitable for this recipe. This soup is suitable to freeze. Top with dip and almonds after reheating.

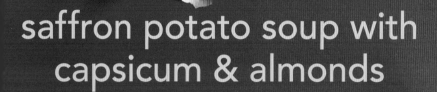

saffron potato soup with capsicum & almonds

- 1 tablespoon extra virgin olive oil
- 2 medium brown onions (300g), chopped finely
- 4 cloves garlic, crushed
- pinch saffron threads
- 5 medium potatoes (1kg), chopped coarsely
- 3 cups (750ml) vegetable stock
- 3 cups (750ml) water
- 2 tablespoons blanched almonds
- ⅔ cup (150g) capsicum (bell pepper) dip

1 Heat oil in a large saucepan over medium heat; cook onion, stirring, until soft. Add garlic and saffron; cook, stirring, until fragrant.

2 Add potato to the pan with stock and the water; simmer, covered, 20 minutes or until soft. Stand 10 minutes.

3 Meanwhile, add nuts to a small frying pan; stir over medium heat until toasted lightly. Cool; chop coarsely.

4 Blend soup in batches until smooth (or use a stick blender).

5 Return soup to the pan; stir over medium heat until hot. Season to taste.

6 Ladle soup into serving bowls; top with dip, nuts and freshly ground black pepper.

serves 4
prep + cook time 40 minutes
nutritional count per serving 11.8g total fat (3.3g saturated fat); 1235kJ (295 cal); 33.3g carbohydrate; 10.1g protein; 6.7g fibre

kumara soup with rosemary sourdough

- 1 tablespoon olive oil
- 2 medium kumara (orange sweet potatoes) (800g), chopped coarsely
- 1 medium brown onion (150g), chopped coarsely
- 2 cloves garlic, quartered
- 2 teaspoons coarsely chopped fresh rosemary
- 1 teaspoon finely grated lemon rind
- 2 cups (500ml) vegetable stock
- 2 cups (500ml) water
- 1 tablespoon lemon juice
- ½ cup (125ml) pouring cream

rosemary sourdough

- 2 tablespoons olive oil
- 2 teaspoons finely chopped fresh rosemary
- 1 loaf sourdough bread (675g), cut into 3cm (1¼-inch) slices

1 Heat oil in a large saucepan; cook kumara, onion and garlic, stirring, 10 minutes. Add rosemary, rind, stock and the water; bring to the boil. Reduce heat; simmer, covered, 15 minutes or until kumara is soft. Cool 15 minutes.

2 Meanwhile, make rosemary sourdough.

3 Blend or process soup, in batches, until smooth. Return soup to same cleaned pan, add juice; stir over medium heat until hot. Season to taste.

4 Serve bowls of soup drizzled with cream, accompanied with rosemary sourdough.

rosemary sourdough

Preheat oven to 180°C/350°F. Combine oil and rosemary in a small bowl. Place bread on an oven tray; brush both sides with olive oil mixture. Bake bread slices, 15 minutes, turning halfway, until toasted and golden.

serves 6
prep + cook time
40 minutes (+ cooling)
nutritional count per serving 21g total fat (7.8g saturated fat); 2257kJ (540 cal); 69.1g carbohydrate; 15.7g protein; 5.6g fibre

tips Soup can be made up to two days ahead; store, covered, in the refrigerator. The soup is equally delicious served with thick slices of fresh sourdough.

serves 4
prep + cook time 40 minutes
**nutritional count per
serving** 42.4g total fat
(15.6g saturated fat); 2504kJ
(599 cal); 14.6g carbohydrate;
38.4g protein; 5.5g fibre

white bean & merguez soup with gremolata

- 1 tablespoon olive oil
- 1 medium red onion (170g), chopped coarsely
- 2 rindless bacon slices (130g), chopped coarsely
- 2 cloves garlic, crushed
- 400g (12½ ounces) canned diced tomatoes
- 1.5 litres (6 cups) chicken stock
- 6 merguez sausages (480g)
- 800g (1½ pounds) canned white beans, rinsed, drained

gremolata

- ⅓ cup finely chopped fresh flat-leaf parsley
- 2 teaspoons finely grated lemon rind
- 2 cloves garlic, crushed

1 Heat olive oil in a large saucepan over medium heat. Add onion, bacon and garlic, cook, stirring, 8 minutes or until onion softens and bacon crisps. Add tomatoes and stock; bring to a boil. Reduce heat; simmer, uncovered, 20 minutes, stirring occasionally.

2 Meanwhile, cook sausages in a heated oiled medium fry pan, turning, 8 minutes or until browned and cooked through; slice thinly.

3 Add sausage to soup with beans; stir until soup is hot.

4 Make gremolata. Serve bowls of soup sprinkled with gremolata.

gremolata Combine ingredients in a small bowl.

tips Merguez is a small spicy lamb sausage eaten in Tunisia and Algeria, available from selected butchers. You could substitute fresh chorizo sausages if merguez are unavailable.

corn soup with parmesan crisps & chilli

- 8 cobs trimmed corn (2kg)
- 30g (1 ounce) butter
- 1 large brown onion (200g), chopped finely
- 2 cups (500ml) vegetable stock
- 1 cup (250ml) water
- 1 cup (250ml) thickened (heavy) cream
- 1 tablespoon vegetable oil
- 1 fresh long red chilli, sliced thinly
- ⅔ cup (10g) puffed corn
- baby coriander (cilantro) leaves

parmesan crisps
- ⅓ cup (25g) finely grated parmesan

serves 4
prep + cook time 40 minutes
nutritional count per serving 40.1g total fat (20.7g saturated fat); 2503kJ (598 cal); 37.6g carbohydrate; 15.2g protein; 15.1g fibre

1 Cut kernels from corn cobs.
2 Heat butter in a large saucepan over medium heat; cook onion, stirring, until soft but not coloured. Add stock and the water; bring to the boil. Add corn kernels; simmer, covered, 20 minutes or until corn is tender. Stand 10 minutes.
3 Meanwhile, make parmesan crisps.
4 Blend half the soup mixture until smooth; return to the pan. Stir in cream over medium heat until hot. Season to taste.
5 Heat oil in a small frying pan; cook chilli, stirring, until soft.
6 Ladle soup into serving bowls; top with puffed corn, chilli and the oil, then coriander. Serve with parmesan crisps.
parmesan crisps Preheat oven to 180°C/350°F. Line a large oven tray with baking paper. Sprinkle parmesan in a thin layer on tray; flatten slightly. Bake 8 minutes or until browned lightly. Cool on tray. Break into pieces when cold.

tip You can use 1.6kg (11 cups) frozen corn kernels to save time.

serves 8
prep + cook time 40 minutes
nutritional count per serving
17.2g total fat (10.9g saturated fat);
1141.5kJ (272 cal); 17g carbohydrate;
10g protein; 4.2g fibre

spinach soup with fetta

- 40g (1½ ounces) butter
- 1 medium brown onion (150g), chopped coarsely
- 4 green onions (scallions), chopped coarsely
- 2 cloves garlic, quartered
- 1 tablespoon coarsely grated lemon rind
- 1.5kg (3¼ pounds) spinach, trimmed, chopped coarsely
- 3 large potatoes (900g), chopped coarsely
- 3 cups (750ml) vegetable stock
- 5 cups (1.25 litres) water
- ¾ cup (180ml) pouring cream
- 150g (5 ounces) fetta, crumbled

1 Melt butter in a large saucepan; cook onions and garlic, stirring, for 5 minutes or until onion softens. Add rind, spinach and potato; cook, stirring, until spinach is just wilted.
2 Stir in stock and the water. Bring to the boil; simmer, covered, 15 minutes or until potato softens.
3 Stand 10 minutes then blend or process soup mixture, in batches, until smooth.
4 Return soup, with cream, to same cleaned pan; stir over heat until hot. Ladle soup into bowls; top each with fetta.

- 1 tablespoon olive oil
- 1 large brown onion (200g), chopped finely
- 2 sticks celery (300g) trimmed, chopped coarsely
- 2 medium carrots (240g), chopped coarsely
- 3 cloves garlic, crushed
- 1 teaspoon dried oregano
- ¼ teaspoon dried chilli flakes
- 1 litre (4 cups) boiling water
- 1 litre (4 cups) salt-reduced vegetable stock
- 125g tagliatelle
- ¼ cup coarsely chopped fresh flat-leaf parsley
- 60g (2 ounces) baby spinach leaves, torn

1 Heat oil in a large saucepan over medium heat; cook onion, celery, carrot, garlic, oregano and chilli, stirring, 8 minutes or until vegetables are just tender.

2 Add the boiling water and stock to the pan; bring to the boil. Add pasta, reduce heat; simmer, uncovered, stirring occasionally, 12 minutes or until pasta is tender. Stir in parsley.

3 Divide spinach between bowls; ladle soup over the top.

tip Tagliatelle are long, flat strips of wheat pasta, slightly narrower and thinner than fettuccine.

vegetable & pasta soup

serves 4
prep + cook time
40 minutes
nutritional count per
serving 6.2g total fat
(1.2g saturated fat);
861kJ (206 cal);
29.2g carbohydrate;
8.3g protein; 5g fibre

serves 4
prep + cook time
40 minutes
nutritional count per
serving 7.6g total fat
(1.4g saturated fat);
836kJ (200 cal);
16.6g carbohydrate;
12.6g protein; 8.2g fibre

mushroom & chickpea soup

- 1 tablespoon olive oil
- 1 medium brown onion (150g), chopped finely
- 2 cloves garlic, crushed
- 200g (6½ ounces) button mushrooms, sliced thinly
- 200g (6½ ounces) swiss brown mushrooms, sliced thinly
- 1 litre (4 cups) chicken stock
- 400g (12½ ounces) canned chickpeas, (garbanzo beans) rinsed, drained
- 400g (12½ ounces) canned crushed tomatoes
- 100g (3 ounces) baby spinach leaves

1 Heat oil in a large saucepan over medium heat; cook onion and garlic, stirring, 5 minutes or until onion softens.
2 Add mushrooms; cook, stirring, 5 minutes or until tender. Add stock, chickpeas and tomatoes; bring to the boil. Reduce heat; simmer, covered, 20 minutes.
3 Stir in spinach; serve soup as soon as spinach wilts.

creamy pumpkin & potato soup

- 1 tablespoon olive oil
- 1 medium brown onion (150g), chopped coarsely
- 1 clove garlic, crushed
- 600g (1¼ pounds) pumpkin, chopped coarsely
- 2 medium potatoes (400g), chopped coarsely
- 2 cups (500ml) water
- 1½ cups (375ml) vegetable stock
- ½ cup (125ml) pouring cream
- 1 tablespoon lemon juice

garlic & chive croûtons
- ⅓ loaf ciabatta (150g)
- 2 tablespoons olive oil
- 1 clove garlic, crushed
- 1 tablespoon finely chopped fresh chives

1 Heat oil in a large saucepan over medium heat; cook onion and garlic, stirring, 5 minutes or until onion softens. Add pumpkin, potato, the water and stock; bring to the boil. Reduce heat; simmer, covered, 20 minutes or until vegetables are tender.
2 Meanwhile, make garlic and chive croûtons.
3 Blend or process soup, in batches, until smooth. Return soup to same pan; add cream and juice. Reheat, stirring, without boiling, until hot.
4 Serve bowls of soup topped with garlic & chive croûtons.

garlic & chive croûtons
Preheat oven to 180°C/350°F. Cut bread into 2cm (¾-inch) cubes; combine bread in a large bowl with oil, garlic and chives. Place bread on an oven tray; bake, turning occasionally, 12 minutes or until golden and toasted.

serves 4
prep + cook time 35 minutes
nutritional count per serving 29.3g total fat (11.7g saturated fat); 2006kJ (480 cal); 41.4g carbohydrate; 10.7g protein; 5g fibre

beef dumpling soup

- 1.5 litres (6 cups) water
- 2 cups (500ml) beef stock
- 10cm (4-inch) stalk lemon grass (20g), halved lengthways
- 2 kaffir lime leaves
- 1 tablespoon light soy sauce
- 1 tablespoon lime juice
- 500g (1 pound) baby buk choy, chopped coarsely
- 1 cup (80g) bean sprouts
- ¼ cup loosely packed fresh coriander (cilantro) leaves
- 1 red bird's-eye chilli, sliced finely

beef dumplings

- 185g (6 ounces) minced (ground) beef
- 2.5cm (1-inch) piece ginger (10g), grated
- 1 clove garlic, crushed
- 1 tablespoon finely chopped fresh coriander (cilantro)
- 1 tablespoon light soy sauce
- 1 red bird's-eye chilli, chopped finely
- 20 gow gee wrappers

1 Make beef dumplings.

2 Combine the water, stock, lemon grass and lime leaves in a large saucepan; bring to the boil. Reduce heat; simmer broth, uncovered, 15 minutes. Discard lemon grass and lime leaves.

3 Return broth to the boil; add dumplings. Simmer, uncovered, 5 minutes or until dumplings are cooked through. Stir in soy sauce and lime juice.

4 Divide buk choy between bowls; ladle hot broth and dumplings over the top. Serve with bean sprouts, coriander and chilli.

beef dumplings

Combine mince, ginger, garlic, coriander, sauce and chilli in a medium bowl. Place rounded teaspoons of mince mixture in the centre of each gow gee wrapper. Brush edges with water; pinch points of wrappers together to completely enclose filling and seal.

serves 4
prep + cook time 40 minutes
nutritional count per serving 5.4g total fat (2.1g saturated fat); 1062kJ (254 cal); 31g carbohydrate; 18g protein; 3.7g fibre

spiced carrot soup with smoked almonds

- 1 tablespoon extra virgin olive oil
- 2 medium brown onions (300g), chopped coarsely
- 4cm (1½-inch) piece fresh ginger (20g), grated finely
- 2 teaspoons ground cumin
- 1 teaspoon ground coriander
- ½ cinnamon stick
- 1kg (2 pounds) carrots, cut into 1cm (½-inch) slices
- 2 cups (500ml) vegetable stock
- 3 cups (750ml) water
- ¾ cup (200g) greek-style yoghurt
- 2 cloves garlic, crushed
- ½ small red onion (50g), sliced thinly lengthways
- ¼ cup (40g) chopped smoked almonds
- 8 sprigs fresh coriander (cilantro)

1 Heat oil in a large saucepan over medium heat; cook brown onion, stirring, until soft.

2 Add ginger, cumin, ground coriander and cinnamon to the pan; cook, stirring, until fragrant. Add carrot, stock and the water; bring to the boil. Reduce heat; simmer, covered, 20 minutes or until soft. Remove cinnamon stick. Stand soup 10 minutes.

3 Meanwhile, combine yoghurt and garlic in a small bowl.

4 Blend soup in batches until smooth. Return soup to same cleaned pan; stir over medium heat until hot; season.

5 Ladle soup into serving bowls; top with yoghurt mixture, red onion, nuts and fresh coriander.

serves 4
prep + cook time 40 minutes
nutritional count per serving 14.5g total fat (3.3g saturated fat); 1190kJ (284 cal); 24g carbohydrate; 8.9g protein; 11.7g fibre

60 minutes

These recipes take a little longer, so are perfect for cooking on the weekend. Try italian seafood stew or barley & vegetable soup with crunchy seeds — they'll cure anyone's winter blues.

italian seafood stew

- 1 tablespoon olive oil
- 1 medium brown onion (150g), chopped finely
- 3 cloves garlic, crushed
- 700g (1½ pounds) tomato passata
- 1½ cups (375ml) fish stock
- ½ cup (125ml) dry white wine
- 2 strips lemon rind
- 600g (1¼ pounds) uncooked medium king prawns
- 600g (1¼ pounds) firm white fish fillets
- 300g (9½ ounces) clams, scrubbed
- 12 scallops without roe (300g)
- ¼ cup finely shredded fresh basil
- ¼ cup coarsely chopped fresh flat-leaf parsley

1 Heat oil in a large saucepan over medium heat; cook onion and garlic, stirring, 5 minutes or until onion softens. Add passata, stock, wine and rind; bring to the boil. Reduce heat; simmer, covered, 20 minutes.

2 Meanwhile, shell and devein prawns, leaving tails intact. Cut fish into 2cm (¾-inch) pieces.

3 Add clams to pan; cook, covered, 5 minutes. Discard any clams that do not open. Add prawns, fish and scallops to pan; cook, covered, stirring occasionally, 5 minutes or until seafood just changes colour. Stir in herbs.

serves 4
prep + cook time
1 hour 10 minutes
nutritional count per
serving 9.4g total fat
(2g saturated fat);
1772kJ (424 cal);
14.5g carbohydrate;
62g protein; 4.7g fibre

tip Not suitable to freeze.

french onion soup

- 40g (1½ ounces) butter
- 3 large brown onions (600g), sliced thinly
- 1 tablespoon finely chopped fresh thyme
- ⅓ cup (80ml) dry white wine
- 1 tablespoon plain (all-purpose) flour
- 1 litre (4 cups) salt-reduced beef stock
- 1 small white bread roll (50g), ends trimmed, cut into 6 slices
- 1⅓ cup (40g) finely grated gruyère cheese

1 Heat butter in a large non-stick saucepan over medium heat; cook onion and thyme, stirring, 20 minutes or until onion is caramelised. Add wine; bring to the boil. Add flour; cook, stirring, until mixture bubbles and thickens. Gradually add stock; cook, stirring, until mixture boils and thickens. Reduce heat; simmer, uncovered, 15 minutes. Season to taste.

2 Meanwhile, preheat grill (broiler). Place bread on an oven tray; grill until browned lightly each side. Sprinkle cheese over one side of each toast; grill until cheese melts.

3 Serve soup topped with cheese toasts.

tip Reheat soup in the microwave on HIGH (100%) for about 1½ minutes, stirring halfway through heating.

serves 2
prep + cook time
45 minutes
nutritional count per
serving 7.5g total fat
(4.4g saturated fat);
1421kJ (340 cal);
36.6g carbohydrate;
22.1g protein; 4.9g fibre

serves 4
prep + cook time 1 hour
nutritional count per
serving 63.9g total fat
(41.6g saturated fat);
3478kJ (832 cal);
25g carbohydrate;
38g protein; 6.8g fibre

coconut, chicken & kaffir lime soup

- 1 tablespoon peanut oil
- 600g (1¼ pounds) chicken thigh fillets, cut into 1cm (½ inch) strips
- ¼ cup (75g) green curry paste
- 1 litre (4 cups) chicken stock
- 3¼ cups (800ml) coconut milk
- 1 long green chilli, chopped finely
- 8 kaffir lime leaves, shredded
- 125g rice vermicelli
- 2 tablespoons grated palm sugar
- 2 tablespoons lime juice
- 2 tablespoons fish sauce
- 1 cup (80g) bean sprouts
- ½ cup loosely packed vietnamese mint leaves
- 1 long green chilli, sliced thinly
- 2 limes, cut into thin wedges

1 Heat oil in a large saucepan over medium heat; cook chicken, in batches, 5 minutes or until browned lightly. Remove from pan.

2 Place paste in same pan; cook, stirring, until fragrant. Return chicken to pan with stock, coconut milk, chopped chilli and lime leaves; bring to the boil. Reduce heat; simmer, uncovered, 30 minutes, skimming fat from surface occasionally. Add vermicelli; cook, uncovered, until vermicelli is just tender. Stir in sugar, juice and sauce.

3 Serve soup sprinkled with sprouts, mint, sliced chilli and lime.

tips Aromatic fresh kaffir lime leaves are used similarly to bay or curry leaves in the food of South-East Asia. Sold fresh, dried or frozen, they look like two glossy dark-green leaves joined end to end, forming a rounded hourglass shape. While readily available in most greengrocers and many supermarkets, you can use washed lemon or lime tree leaves instead.

minestrone

- 2 teaspoons olive oil
- 1 medium brown onion (150g), chopped finely
- 2 cloves garlic, crushed
- 1 stick celery (150g), trimmed, chopped coarsely
- 1 large carrot (180g), chopped coarsely
- 1 litre (4 cups) vegetable stock
- 1 cup (250ml) water
- 800g (1½ pounds) canned crushed tomatoes
- 1 medium zucchini (120g), chopped coarsely
- 2 cups (160g) finely shredded cabbage
- 150g (4½ ounces) small shell pasta
- 300g (9½ ounces) canned white beans, rinsed, drained
- ¼ cup coarsely chopped fresh flat-leaf parsley
- ¾ cup (60g) shaved parmesan

1 Heat oil in a large saucepan; cook onion and garlic, stirring, until onion softens. Add celery and carrot; cook, stirring, 5 minutes.

2 Stir in stock, the water and undrained tomatoes; bring to the boil. Reduce heat; simmer, covered, about 20 minutes or until vegetables are tender.

3 Add zucchini, cabbage, pasta and beans; cook, uncovered, about 15 minutes or until pasta is tender. Stir in parsley.

4 Serve soup topped with cheese, and crusty bread if you like.

serves 6
prep + cook time 1 hour
nutritional count per serving 6.2g total fat (2.7g saturated fat); 949kJ (227 cal); 29.7g carbohydrate; 12.7g protein; 7g fibre

tip This soup, without seed topping, can be frozen for up to 3 months. Add a little extra water on reheating, if needed.

barley & vegetable soup with crunchy seeds

- 2 tablespoons extra virgin olive oil
- 1 large red onion (300g), chopped coarsely
- 1 medium parsnip (250g), chopped coarsely
- 2 sticks celery (300g), trimmed, chopped coarsely
- 4 cloves garlic, chopped finely
- 1 cup (250ml) bottled tomato pasta sauce (passata)
- 1 litre (4 cups) vegetable stock
- 1 litre (4 cups) water
- 2 medium red capsicums (bell peppers) (400g), chopped coarsely

- 400g (12½ ounces) canned cannellini beans, drained, rinsed
- ½ cup (100g) pearl barley or spelt, rinsed
- 2 tablespoons pepitas (pumpkin seed kernels)
- 2 tablespoons sunflower seeds
- 2 tablespoons drained baby capers, rinsed
- 2 tablespoons dried currants
- ¼ cup loosely packed torn fresh basil leaves
- ½ cup (40g) finely grated parmesan

1 Heat half the oil in a large saucepan over medium heat; cook onion, parsnip, celery and garlic, stirring, 5 minutes or until softened.

2 Add sauce, stock and the water; bring to the boil. Stir in capsicum, beans and barley; simmer, covered, 25 minutes or until barley is tender. Season to taste.

3 Meanwhile, heat remaining oil in a small frying pan over medium heat; cook pepitas, seeds and capers, stirring, until browned lightly and fragrant. Add currants; stir until combined.

4 Just before serving, stir basil into soup. Ladle soup into serving bowls; sprinkle with seed mixture and parmesan.

serves 6
prep + cook time 45 minutes
nutritional count
per serving 11.1g total fat
(2.7g saturated fat);
1244kJ (298 cal);
34.2g carbohydrate;
11.8g protein; 9.2g fibre

barbecued pork in orange & tamarind broth

- 20g (½ ounce) dried shiitake mushrooms
- 2 teaspoons vegetable oil
- 4 shallots (100g), chopped finely
- 1 clove garlic, crushed
- 2 red bird's-eye chillies, chopped finely
- 2 litres (8 cups) water
- 1 litre (4 cups) beef stock
- 2 teaspoons finely grated orange rind
- ¼ cup (60ml) orange juice
- 1 tablespoon tamarind concentrate
- 400g (14 ounces) chinese barbecued pork, sliced thinly
- 100g (3 ounces) swiss brown mushrooms, sliced thinly
- 4 green onions (scallions), sliced thinly

1 Place dried mushrooms in a small bowl, cover with cold water; stand 1 hour. Drain; remove stems, slice thinly.

2 Meanwhile, heat oil in a large saucepan; cook shallot, garlic and chilli, stirring, 5 minutes or until shallot softens. Add the water, stock, rind, juice and tamarind; bring to the boil. Add pork, shiitake and swiss brown mushrooms; reduce heat, simmer, covered, 10 minutes or until soup is hot.

3 Serve bowls of soup sprinkled with onion.

serves 8
prep + cook time 45 minutes (+ standing)
nutritional count per serving 9.1g total fat (3.4g saturated fat); 648kJ (155 cal); 4.3g carbohydrate; 13.1g protein; 2.1g fibre

tip Chinese barbecued pork is roasted pork fillet with a sweet, sticky coating. It is available from Asian grocery stores or specialty food shops.

serves 4
prep + cook time 1 hour
**nutritional count per
serving** 9g total fat
(1.3g saturated fat); 849kJ
(203 cal); 3.9g carbohydrate;
25.2g protein; 2.3g fibre

tom yum goong

- **900g (1¾ pounds) uncooked large king prawns**
- **1 tablespoon peanut oil**
- **1.5 litres (6 cups) water**
- **2 tablespoons red curry paste**
- **1 tablespoon tamarind concentrate**
- **10cm stalk lemon grass (20g), chopped finely**
- **1 teaspoon ground turmeric**
- **2 fresh small red thai chillies, chopped coarsely**
- **1cm piece fresh ginger (5g), grated**
- **6 kaffir lime leaves, shredded finely**
- **1 teaspoon grated palm sugar**
- **100g (3 ounces) shiitake mushrooms, halved**
- **2 tablespoons fish sauce**
- **2 tablespoons lime juice**
- **¼ cup loosely packed fresh vietnamese mint leaves**
- **¼ cup loosely packed fresh coriander leaves**

1 Shell and devein prawns, leaving tails intact; reserve heads and shells.

2 Heat oil in a large saucepan over medium heat; cook reserved prawn shells and heads, stirring, 5 minutes or until deep orange in colour.

3 Add 1 cup of the water and curry paste to pan; bring to the boil, stirring. Add remaining water; return to the boil. Reduce heat; simmer, uncovered, 20 minutes. Strain broth through a fine sieve into a large heatproof bowl; discard solids.

4 Return broth to same cleaned pan. Add tamarind, lemon grass, turmeric, chilli, ginger, lime leaves and sugar; bring to the boil. Boil, stirring, 2 minutes. Add mushrooms, reduce heat to low-medium; cook, stirring, 3 minutes. Add prawns; cook 5 minutes or until prawns are just cooked through. Remove from heat; stir in sauce and juice.

5 Serve bowls of soup sprinkled with mint and coriander.

tip To make fried polenta, cook 1 cup instant polenta and 3½ cups water, following packet instructions. Stir in 20g (¾ ounce) butter and 1 cup finely grated parmesan. Spoon into a baking-paper-lined 20cm x 30cm (8-inch x 12-inch) slice pan. Chill to set. Turn out, cut into 18 fingers. Shallow-fry in hot oil until golden.

roasted capsicum soup

- 4 medium red capsicums (bell peppers) (800g)
- 2 cloves garlic, unpeeled
- 1 tablespoon olive oil
- 1 medium brown onion (150g), chopped finely
- 1 teaspoon sweet paprika
- 3 cups (750ml) water
- 1 litre (4 cups) chicken stock
- ½ cup (125ml) pouring cream
- 2 teaspoons white sugar
- 1 tablespoon finely chopped fresh chives

serves 6
prep + cook time 1 hour (+ cooling)
nutritional count per serving 12.7g total fat (6.5g saturated fat); 727kJ (174 cal); 9.9g carbohydrate; 4.1g protein; 2.6g fibre

1 Quarter capsicums, discard seeds and membranes. Roast capsicum and garlic under grill (broiler) or in a very hot oven, skin-side up, until skin blisters and blackens. Cover capsicum pieces in plastic or paper for 5 minutes, peel away skin. Peel garlic; chop coarsely.
2 Heat oil in a large saucepan; cook onion, stirring, until softened. Add paprika; cook, stirring, until fragrant.
3 Add the water, stock, capsicum and garlic; bring to a boil. Reduce heat; simmer, uncovered, 40 minutes. Cool 15 minutes.
4 Blend or process soup, in batches, until smooth. Return soup to same cleaned pan, add cream and sugar; stir over medium heat until hot.
5 Serve bowls of soup sprinkled with chives.
serving suggestion Serve with fried polenta or crusty bread.

harissa soup
with chickpeas

- 2 large red capsicums (bell peppers) (700g)
- 1 tablespoon olive oil
- ½ teaspoon ground turmeric
- ½ teaspoon ground cinnamon
- ¾ teaspoon ground ginger
- ¾ teaspoon ground cumin
- 2 cloves garlic, chopped coarsely
- 4 long red chillies, chopped coarsely
- 1 red bird's-eye chilli, chopped coarsely
- 2 medium tomatoes (300g), chopped coarsely
- 1½ cups (375ml) chicken or vegetable stock
- 2 x 3cm (1¼-inch) strips lemon rind
- 400g (12½ ounces) canned chickpeas (garbanzo beans)

cumin-spiced yoghurt
- 1 teaspoon cumin seeds
- ⅓ cup (95g) greek-style yoghurt
- ½ teaspoon finely grated lemon rind

1 Preheat grill (broiler).
2 Quarter capsicums; discard seeds and membranes. Cook under grill (broiler), skin-side up, until skin blisters and blackens. Cover capsicum pieces with plastic or paper for 5 minutes; peel away skin, then chop capsicum coarsely.
3 Meanwhile, heat oil in a large saucepan over medium heat; add spices. Cook, stirring, until fragrant. Add garlic, chillies, tomato and capsicum; cook, stirring, 5 minutes. Add stock and rind; bring to the boil. Reduce heat, simmer, covered, 10 minutes; season to taste. Cool 10 minutes. Discard rind.

4 Meanwhile, make cumin-spiced yoghurt.
5 Blend soup until smooth. Return soup to pan; add rinsed and drained chickpeas. Stir soup over medium heat until hot. Serve with cumin-spiced yoghurt.
cumin-spiced yoghurt
Heat seeds in a small dry frying pan until fragrant. Remove from heat. Combine seeds, yoghurt and rind in a small bowl.

serves 4
prep + cook time 50 minutes
nutritional count per serving 2.3g total fat (0.7g saturated fat); 216kJ (52 cal); 4.6g carbohydrate; 2.2g protein; 1.9g fibre

ribollita

- ⅓ cup (80ml) olive oil
- 1 small brown onion (80g), chopped coarsely
- 1 trimmed stick celery (150g), chopped coarsely
- 1 medium carrot (120g), chopped coarsely
- 100g (3 ounces) sliced prosciutto
- 2 medium tomatoes (300g), chopped coarsely
- 3 cloves garlic, crushed
- 1 litre (4 cups) water or chicken stock
- 1 cinnamon stick
- 1 sprig rosemary
- 300g (9½ ounces) loaf olive bread
- 200g (6½ ounces) cavolo nero
- 125g (4 ounces) green beans, chopped coarsely
- 400g (12½ ounces) canned cannellini beans, rinse, drained
- ¾ cup (60g) shaved parmesan

1 Preheat oven to 200°C/400°F.

2 Heat 1 tablespoon of the oil in a large saucepan, add onion, celery and carrot. Chop half the prosciutto, add to pan; cook, stirring, 8 minutes or until vegetables are soft. Add tomato and half the garlic; cook, stirring, until soft. Add the water, cinnamon and rosemary; bring to the boil, simmer, uncovered, 10 minutes. Discard cinnamon and rosemary.

3 Meanwhile, tear bread into chunks; toss with remaining garlic and oil on an oven tray; season. Place remaining prosciutto on a wire rack over an oven tray. Bake prosciutto 5 minutes and bread about 10 minutes or until prosciutto is crisp and bread is golden. Break prosciutto into pieces.

4 Remove stalks from cavolo nero; chop leaves coarsely.

5 Add green beans to soup; simmer, uncovered, 5 minutes. Add cavolo nero and cannellini beans to pan; simmer, uncovered a further 5 minutes or until tender.

6 Serve soup topped with toasted bread, crisp prosciutto and cheese.

tips Ribollita is a Tuscan soup based on whatever vegetable the cook has at hand. Traditionally, it is thickened with stale bread. Our version uses chunky garlic breadcrumbs, which add some crunch. Cavolo nero is also known as tuscan kale or black cabbage.

serves 4
prep + cook time
45 minutes (+ cooling)
**nutritional count per
serving** 26.7g total fat
(5.1g saturated fat);
2189kJ (523 cal);
43.9g carbohydrate;
21.2g protein; 11.5g fibre

chicken stock

- 2kg (4 pounds) chicken bones
- 2 medium onions (300g), chopped coarsely
- 2 trimmed celery sticks (200g), chopped coarsely
- 2 medium carrots (240g), chopped coarsely
- 3 dried bay leaves
- 2 teaspoons black peppercorns
- 5 litres (20 cups) water

1 Combine ingredients in a large saucepan or boiler; simmer, uncovered, 2 hours, skimming surface occasionally.
2 Strain stock through a fine sieve into a large heatproof bowl; discard solids. Allow stock to cool, cover; refrigerate until cold. Skim and discard surface fat before using.

makes 3.5 litres
prep + cook time 2 hours 10 minutes (+ cooling & refrigeration)
nutritional count per 1 cup (250ml) 0.6g total fat (0.2g saturated fat); 105kJ (25 cal); 2.3g carbohydrate; 1.9g protein; 1.1g fibre

fish stock

- 1.5kg white-fleshed fish bones
- 1 medium onion (150g), chopped coarsely
- 2 trimmed celery sticks (200g), chopped coarsely
- 2 dried bay leaves
- 1 teaspoon black peppercorns
- 3 litres (12 cups) water

1 Combine ingredients in a large saucepan; simmer gently, uncovered, 20 minutes.
2 Strain stock through a fine sieve into a large heatproof bowl; discard solids. Allow stock to cool, cover; refrigerate until cold. Skim and discard surface fat before using.

makes 2.5 litres
prep + cook time 30 minutes (+ cooling & refrigeration)
nutritional count per 1 cup (250 ml) 0.2g total fat (0.1g saturated fat); 63kJ (15 cal); 1.1g carbohydrate; 1.9g protein; 0.6g fibre

vegetable stock

- 2 large carrots (360g),
  chopped coarsely
- 2 large parsnips (700g),
  chopped coarsely
- 4 medium onions (600g),
  chopped coarsely
- 10 trimmed celery sticks (1kg),
  chopped coarsely
- 4 dried bay leaves
- 2 teaspoons black peppercorns
- 6 litres (24 cups) water

1 Combine ingredients in a large saucepan; simmer, uncovered, 1½ hours.
2 Strain stock through a fine sieve into a large heatproof bowl; discard solids.

makes 3.5 litres
prep + cook time 1 hour 40 minutes
nutritional count per 1 cup (250ml)
0.2g total fat (0g saturated fat);
151kJ (36 cal); 5.7g carbohydrate;
1.4g protein; 2.9g fibre

COOLING

Before you freeze a soup, cool it so it doesn't damage your freezer. For food safety reasons, it's best to do this as rapidly as possible. Either cool slightly at room temperature, then cover and place in the fridge until cooled completely. Or, fill a sink with water and ice cubes and place the pot in it, stir for 1 minute to release the steam, then continue stirring.

FREEZING

Most soups can be frozen successfully for up to 3 months. Exceptions are those that include seafood, dairy (yoghurt, cream, buttermilk), coconut milk/cream, pieces of potato or mushroom and other vegetables with a high water content.

THAWING

If you intend to reheat the soup on the stove, thaw it completely in the fridge first (this takes about 8 hours). Or, you can thaw in the microwave, partially covering the soup, using a defrost setting, stirring at intervals occasionally until thawed.

KEEPING

In the refrigerator, seafood soup should keep for 1 day, chicken-based soup for 2 days, red meat soup for 3 days and vegetable soup for 3 days. Always ensure that the soup comes to the boil before eating.

BAMBOO SHOOTS the tender shoots of bamboo plants, available in cans; must be rinsed and drained before use.

BARLEY a nutritious grain used in soups and stews. Hulled barley, the least processed, is high in fibre. Pearl barley has had the husk removed then been steamed and polished so that only the "pearl" of the original grain remains, much the same as white rice.

BEANS

cannellini a small white bean similar in appearance and flavour to other white beans (great northern, navy or haricot), all of which can be substituted for the other. Available dried or canned.

green also known as french or string beans (although the tough string they once had has generally been bred out of them), this long thin fresh bean is consumed in its entirety once cooked.

lima also known as butter beans; large, flat, kidney-shaped bean, off-white in colour, with a mealy texture and mild taste.

white a generic term we use for canned or cannellini, haricot, navy or great northern beans belonging to the same family, *phaseolus vulgaris*.

BEETROOT (BEETS) also known as red beets; firm, round root vegetable.

BROCCOLINI a cross between broccoli and chinese kale; long asparagus-like stems with a long loose floret, both completely edible. Resembles broccoli but is milder and sweeter in taste.

BUK CHOY also known as bok choy, pak choi, chinese white cabbage or chinese chard; has a fresh, mild mustard taste. Use both stems and leaves. Baby buk choy, also known as *pak kat farang* or shanghai bok choy, is smaller and more tender than buk choy.

BUTTER use salted or unsalted (sweet) butter; 125g is equal to one stick of butter (4 ounces).

CAPERS grey-green buds of a warm climate shrub (usually Mediterranean); sold dried and salted or pickled in a vinegar brine. Rinse before using.

CAPSICUM (BELL PEPPER) Comes in many colours: red, green, yellow, orange and purplish-black. Be sure to discard seeds and membranes before use.

CHEESE

fetta Greek in origin; a crumbly textured goat's- or sheep's-milk cheese with a sharp, salty taste. Ripened and stored in salted whey.

goat's made from goat's milk, has an earthy, strong taste; available in both soft and firm textures, in various shapes and sizes, and sometimes rolled in ash or herbs.

parmesan also called parmigiano; is a hard, grainy cow's-milk cheese originating in Italy. Reggiano is the best variety.

CHICKPEAS (GARBANZO BEANS) also called hummus or channa; an irregularly round, sandy-coloured legume. Has a firm texture even after cooking, a floury mouth-feel and robust nutty flavour; available canned or dried (reconstitute for several hours in cold water before use).

CHILLI generally, the smaller the chilli, the hotter it is. Use rubber gloves when seeding and chopping fresh chillies as they can burn your skin. Removing seeds and membranes lessens the heat level.

long available both fresh and dried; a generic term used for any moderately hot, thin, long (6cm/2¼-inch) chilli.

red thai a small, hot, bright red coloured chilli.

CIABATTA in Italian, the word means slipper, which refers to the traditional shape of this popular crusty, open-textured white sourdough bread.

CINNAMON available in pieces (called sticks or quills) and ground into powder; one of the world's most common spices, used as a sweet, fragrant flavouring for both sweet and savoury foods.

COCONUT

milk not the liquid found inside the fruit (coconut water), but the diluted liquid from the second pressing of the white flesh of a mature coconut.

CORIANDER (CILANTRO) also known as pak chee or chinese parsley; a bright-green leafy herb with a pungent flavour. Both the stems and roots of coriander are also used in cooking; wash well before using. Also available ground or as seeds; these should not be substituted for fresh coriander as the tastes are completely different.

CREAM

pouring also known as pure or fresh cream. It has no additives and contains a minimum fat content of 35%.

thickened (heavy) a whipping cream that contains a thickener. It has a minimum fat content of 35%.

CUMIN also known as zeera or comino; has a spicy, nutty flavour.

CURRY LEAVES available fresh or dried and have a mild curry flavour; use like bay leaves.

CURRY PASTES commercially made pastes vary in strengths and flavours. Use whichever one you feel best suits your spice-level tolerance.

green the hottest of the traditional pastes; contains chilli, garlic, onion, salt, lemon grass, spices and galangal.

red a popular curry paste; a hot blend of red chilli, garlic, shallot, lemon grass, salt, galangal, shrimp paste, kaffir lime peel, coriander, cumin and paprika. It is milder than the hotter thai green curry paste.

EGGPLANT also known as aubergine. Ranging in size from tiny to very large and in colour from pale green to deep purple. Can also be purchased char-grilled, packed in oil, in jars.

FENNEL also called finocchio or anise; a white to very pale green-white, firm, crisp, roundish vegetable about 8-12cm in diameter. The bulb has a slightly sweet, anise flavour but the leaves have a much stronger taste. Also the name given to dried seeds that have a licorice flavour.

FLOUR

plain (all-purpose) an all-purpose wheat flour.

self-raising plain flour sifted with baking powder in the proportion of 1 cup flour to 2 teaspoons baking powder.

GAI LAN also known as chinese broccoli, gai larn, *kanah, gai lum* and chinese kale; appreciated more for its stems than its coarse leaves.

GARAM MASALA a blend of spices that includes cardamom, cinnamon, coriander, cloves, fennel and cumin. Black pepper and chilli can be added for heat.

GOW GEE WRAPPERS also called wonton wrappers or spring roll pastry sheets, are found in the refrigerated or freezer section of Asian food shops and many supermarkets. These come in different thicknesses and shapes. Thin wrappers work best in soups, while the thicker ones are best for frying; and the choice of round or square, small or large is dependent on the recipe.

KAFFIR LIME LEAVES also known as *bai magrood*. Aromatic leaves of a citrus tree; two glossy dark green leaves joined end to end, forming a rounded hourglass shape. A strip of fresh lime peel may be substituted for each kaffir lime leaf.

KECAP MANIS a thick soy sauce with added sugar and spices. The sweetness is derived from the addition of molasses or palm sugar.

KUMARA (ORANGE SWEET POTATO) the Polynesian name of an orange-fleshed sweet potato often confused with yam.

LEEK a member of the onion family, the leek resembles a green onion but is much larger and more subtle in flavour. Tender baby or pencil leeks can be eaten whole with minimal cooking but adult leeks are usually trimmed of most of the green tops then chopped or sliced.

LEMON GRASS a tall, clumping, lemon-smelling and -tasting, sharp-edged grass; the white lower part of the stem is used, finely chopped, in cooking.

LENTILS (red, brown, yellow) dried pulses often identified by and named after their colour; also known as dhal.

ONIONS

green (scallions) also known incorrectly, as shallots; an immature onion picked before the bulb has formed. Has a long, bright-green edible stalk.

shallots also called french shallots, golden shallots or eschalots; small, brown-skinned, elongated members of the onion family.

spring have small white bulbs and long, narrow, green-leafed tops.

POLENTA also known as cornmeal; a flour-like cereal made of ground corn (maize). Also the name of the dish made from it.

QUINOA pronounced keen-wa; is a gluten-free grain. It has a delicate, slightly nutty taste and chewy texture.

RISONI small rice-shape pasta; very similar to another small pasta, orzo.

SAFFRON available ground or in strands; imparts a yellow-orange colour to food once infused. The quality can vary greatly; the best is the most expensive spice in the world.

SAMBAL OELEK (also ulek or olek) Indonesian in origin; a salty paste made from ground chillies and vinegar. Found in supermarkets and Asian food stores.

SILVER BEET also known as swiss chard; mistakenly called spinach.

SNOW PEAS also called *mange tout* (eat all). Snow pea tendrils, the growing shoots of the plant, are also available at greengrocers.

snow pea sprouts are the tender new growths of snow peas.

SOY SAUCE made from fermented soya beans. Several variations are available in most supermarkets and Asian food stores. We use japanese soy sauce unless otherwise indicated.

SPINACH also known as english spinach and, incorrectly, silver beet.

SUGAR, BROWN very soft, finely granulated sugar retaining molasses for its characteristic colour and flavour.

SUMAC a purple-red, astringent spice ground from berries growing on shrubs that flourish wild around the mediterranean; adds a tart, lemony flavour to food. Available from spice shops and major supermarkets.

TAHINI a rich, sesame-seed paste, used in most Middle-Eastern cuisines, especially Lebanese, in dips and sauces.

TOMATO

bottled pasta sauce a prepared sauce; a blend of tomatoes, herbs and spices.

canned whole peeled tomatoes in natural juices; available crushed, chopped or diced. Use undrained.

paste triple-concentrated tomato puree used to flavour soups, stews and sauces.

puree canned pureed tomatoes (not tomato paste).

TAMARIND found in Asian food shops. Gives a sweet-sour, slightly astringent taste to marinades, pastes, sauces and dressings.

TAMARIND CONCENTRATE (or paste) the commercial result of the distillation of tamarind juice into a condensed, compacted paste.

TRUSS small vine-ripened tomatoes with vine still attached.

TURMERIC also called kamin; is a rhizome related to galangal and ginger. Must be grated or pounded to release its acrid aroma and pungent flavour. Known for the golden colour it imparts, fresh turmeric can be substituted with the more commonly found dried powder.

WATERCRESS one of the cress family, a large group of peppery greens. Highly perishable, so must be used as soon as possible.

YOGHURT, GREEK-STYLE plain yoghurt strained in a cloth (traditionally muslin) to remove the whey and to give it a creamy consistency.

ZA'ATAR a Middle Eastern herb and spice mixture which varies; always includes thyme, with ground sumac and, usually, toasted sesame seeds.

ZUCCHINI also called courgette; small, pale-green, dark-green or yellow vegetable of the squash family.

conversion chart

measures

One Australian metric measuring cup holds approximately 250ml, one Australian metric tablespoon holds 20ml, one Australian metric teaspoon holds 5ml. The difference between one country's measuring cups and another's is within a 2- or 3-teaspoon variance, and will not affect your cooking results. North America, New Zealand and the United Kingdom use a 15ml tablespoon. All cup and spoon measurements are level. The most accurate way of measuring dry ingredients is to weigh them. When measuring liquids, use a clear glass or plastic jug with metric markings. We use large eggs with an average weight of 60g.

dry measures

METRIC	IMPERIAL
15g	½oz
30g	1oz
60g	2oz
90g	3oz
125g	4oz (¼lb)
155g	5oz
185g	6oz
220g	7oz
250g	8oz (½lb)
280g	9oz
315g	10oz
345g	11oz
375g	12oz (¾lb)
410g	13oz
440g	14oz
470g	15oz
500g	16oz (1lb)
750g	24oz (1½lb)
1kg	32oz (2lb)

liquid measures

METRIC	IMPERIAL
30ml	1 fluid oz
60ml	2 fluid oz
100ml	3 fluid oz
125ml	4 fluid oz
150ml	5 fluid oz
190ml	6 fluid oz
250ml	8 fluid oz
300ml	10 fluid oz
500ml	16 fluid oz
600ml	20 fluid oz
1000ml (1 litre)	1¾ pints

length measures

METRIC	IMPERIAL
3mm	⅛in
6mm	¼in
1cm	½in
2cm	¾in
2.5cm	1in
5cm	2in
6cm	2½in
8cm	3in
10cm	4in
13cm	5in
15cm	6in
18cm	7in
20cm	8in
23cm	9in
25cm	10in
28cm	11in
30cm	12in (1ft)

oven temperatures

These oven temperatures are only a guide for conventional ovens. For fan-forced ovens, check the manufacturer's manual.

	°C (CELSIUS)	°F (FAHRENHEIT)
Very slow	120	250
Slow	150	275-300
Moderately slow	160	325
Moderate	180	350-375
Moderately hot	200	400
Hot	220	425-450
Very hot	240	475

The imperial measurements used in these recipes are approximate only. Measurements for cake pans are approximate only. Using same-shaped cake pans of a similar size should not affect the outcome of your baking. We measure the inside top of the cake pan to determine sizes.

index

Published in 2013 by Bauer Media Books, Sydney

Bauer Media Books are published by Bauer Media Limited

54 Park St, Sydney

GPO Box 4088, Sydney, NSW 2001.

phone (02) 9282 8618; fax (02) 9126 3702

www.awwcookbooks.com.au

MEDIA GROUP

BAUER MEDIA BOOKS

Publishing Director - Gerry Reynolds

Publisher - Sally Wright

Director of Sales, Marketing & Rights - Brian Cearnes

Editorial & Food Director - Pamela Clark

Creative Director - Hieu Chi Nguyen

Food Concept Director - Sophia Young

Published and Distributed in the United Kingdom by Octopus Publishing Group

Endeavour House

189 Shaftesbury Avenue

London WC2H 8JY

United Kingdom

phone (+44)(0)207 632 5400; fax (+44)(0)207 632 5405

info@octopus-publishing.co.uk;

www.octopusbooks.co.uk

Printed by 1010 Printing International Limited, China.

International foreign language rights, Brian Cearnes, Bauer Media Books

bcearnes@bauer-media.com.au

A catalogue record for this book is available from the British Library.

ISBN 978-1-74245-379-8

© Bauer Media Limited 2013

ABN 18 053 273 546